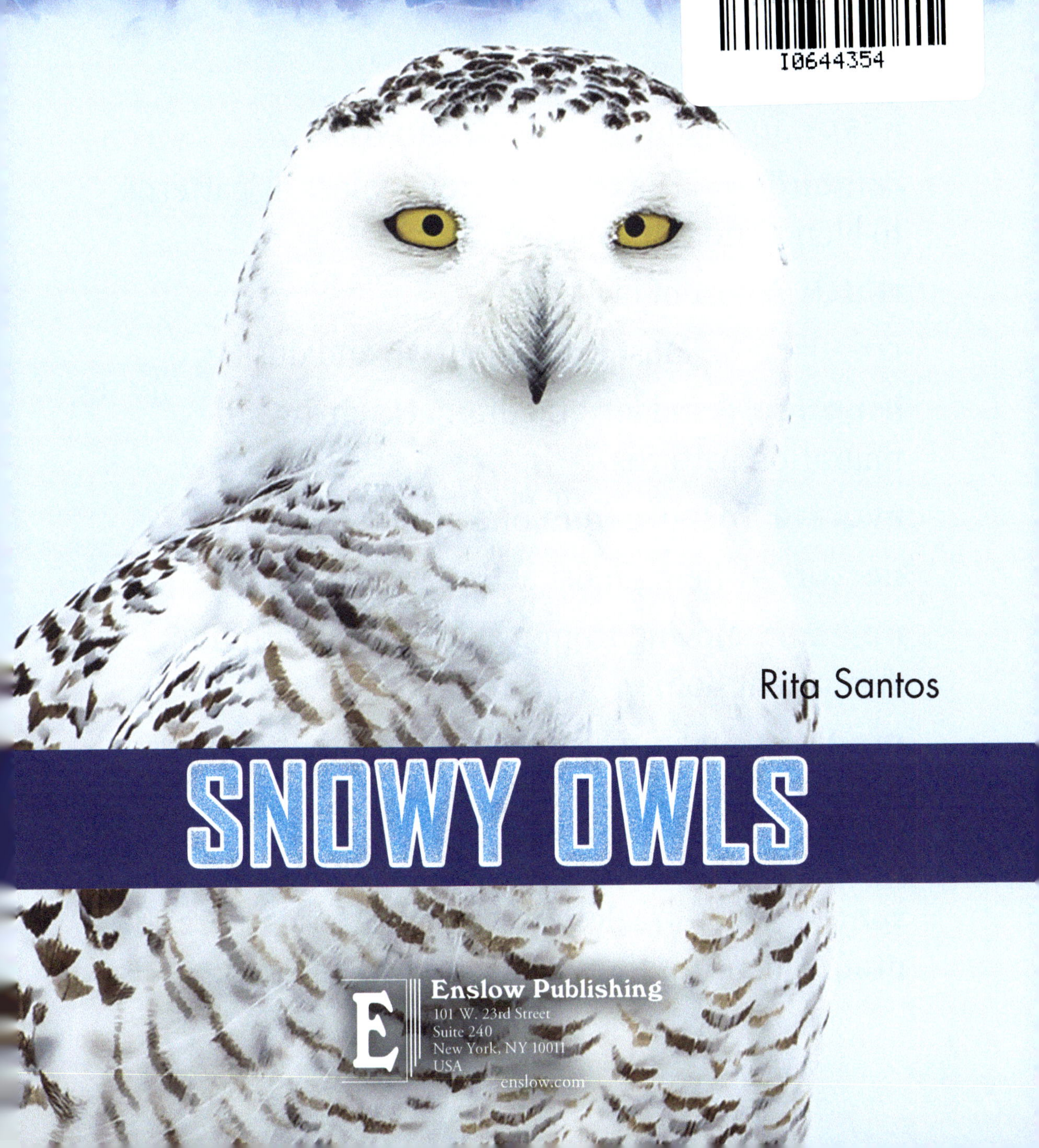

LIFE AT THE POLES

Rita Santos

SNOWY OWLS

Enslow Publishing
101 W. 23rd Street
Suite 240
New York, NY 10011
USA
enslow.com

Words to Know

adapt To change in order to survive.

camouflage The use of certain colors or patterns to blend into the environment.

clutch A nest of owl eggs.

crepuscular Most active at dawn and dusk.

irruption A sudden and dramatic change in migration patterns.

migrate To move from one place to another.

nocturnal Being most active at night.

nomadic Moving from place to place with no permanent home.

predator An animal that hunts another animal.

prey An animal that is hunted by another animal.

talons Sharp claws.

tundra A flat, treeless area of the Arctic where the ground beneath the surface is always frozen.

Contents

1

FRIGID FLIGHTS

Snowy owls are birds of **prey**. They hunt other animals. Snowy owls are the only birds of prey that live in the Arctic **tundra**. It is not hard to see why. It takes a strong animal to survive the bitter cold. In the winter, the average temperature is –30 degrees Fahrenheit (–34 degrees Celsius). Sometimes it drops as low as –58°F (–50°C). Summer isn't much better. Temperatures only rise to

Don't Make Me Mad

Snowy owls click their tongues when they are annoyed.

The snowy owl is at home in the cold Arctic.

54°F (12°C). Snowy owls have **adapted** to this harsh environment.

TRUE OWL

The snowy owl is the largest owl on the continent of North America. Its wings stretch 49 to 59 inches (125 to 150 cm). These owls are usually about 20 to 28 inches (51 to 71 cm) long. They are also one of the heavier owls. They may weigh between 3.5 to 6.6 pounds (1.6 to 3 kg).

Scientists used to think that no other birds were like snowy owls. But now we know that they are related to horned owls. Snowy owls have large **talons** on their feet. They also have thick feathers on their legs and feet to protect them from the cold.

HOME ON THE TUNDRA

Snowy owls, or snowys, are usually found in the tundra. This is an area that includes northern Canada, Alaska, and northern Eurasia. Snowys are **nomadic**. They move

The snowy owl's wings can stretch almost 5 feet (1.5 m) wide.

The tundra is an open area with few trees. It is a good place to hunt.

around a lot. This makes it hard for scientists to study them. Scientists do know that the birds like cold, open spaces. They are often found around airports and beach dunes. It is easier for them to hunt in areas without trees.

2

CATCHING DINNER

Many owls are **nocturnal**. They hunt at night. But in the Arctic summer, the sun never sets. It does not get totally dark. Snowy owls are **crepuscular**. This means that they are most active at dawn and dusk. This is also when their favorite food, lemmings, are most active.

SIT AND WAIT

An adult snowy owl can eat between seven and twelve mice a day. Snowys are very good hunters. They like to find a perch with a good view of the tundra. Their eyes can

A snowy owl flies at sunset. They do most of their hunting when the sun is rising or setting.

see three times better than humans'. Their huge yellow eyes act like binoculars. This means that they can judge distances very well. Their hearing is even better! It is ten times better than human hearing. Snowys hunt their prey mostly by listening for them under the snow. Their wings have special

The snowy owl's main food source is the lemming. These small rodents are related to mice, rats, and hamsters.

feathers that make them almost silent as they swoop down on their prey.

SHARP TALONS

Snowy owls are beautiful, but they are also dangerous birds. They prefer small

Food on the Go

Snowys can catch other birds mid-flight.

mammals that they can eat in one bite. But they have been known to go after larger prey. This might include rabbits, prairie dogs, marmots, and even raccoons.

Adult snowys have few natural **predators**. Not many animals hunt them. This is not true for their eggs and babies. Arctic foxes, grey wolves, skua, and other arctic birds all eat owl eggs and owlets. Snowys will attack anything that comes within a mile of their nest. They dive bomb threats with their sharp talons. A snowy is strong enough to knock down an adult human.

The snowy owl's sharp talons come out as it swoops down towards its prey.

The snowy owl's greatest threat is not another animal. It is a lack of food. Everything from where the owls live to how many eggs they lay at a time is based on their food supply.

3

FOLLOWING LEMMINGS

Snowy owls breed in the summer when the most food is around. First, a male tries to impress a female owl. He brings her a lemming. Then he makes a "V" with his wings and fans his tail feathers. If the female accepts him, the two stay together through the summer. Snowy owls don't nest in trees. Instead they scrape a small hollow in the ground. This is usually on a peak or boulder.

IN THE CLUTCH

Female owls lay about one egg every other day. In five weeks, the eggs begin to hatch

The adult male snowy is mostly white, while the female keeps its dark markings. The birds usually mate for life.

every other day. A group of owl eggs is called a **clutch**. Snowys lay between three and eleven eggs. The size of the clutch depends on how much food is available. When it is very hard to find food, snowys won't nest at all. The mother owl

Handy Beaks

Snowy owls have bristles on their beaks to help them sense nearby prey.

Snowy owls are white when they are born, but they turn brown as new feathers come in.

sits on the owlets for the first 25 days of their life.

OWLETS OUT OF THE NEST

Owlets leave the nest after the first 25 days. Then it takes another 25 days before they can fly well. Owl parents continue to feed their young for five weeks after they leave the nest.

A snowy owl mother and her baby. Both male and female snowys take care of their young.

Every day the male owl must catch lemmings. He needs enough to feed himself and the rest of his family. Growing owlets can eat up to five lemmings a day. Female owls break up the lemmings into bite-sized pieces for the owlets.

4

CHANGING PLANET

In the past few years, snowy owls have started to move away from the Arctic. People have spotted them across the southern United States. There have even been some in Florida. Scientists wondered what was happening. They soon had their answer. The owls were going through an **irruption**.

REASONS FOR IRRUPTION

Many birds **migrate**. They move from place to place as seasons change. In an irruption, the migrating pattern changes a lot. Snowy

A snowy owl rests on a beach on Long Island in New York. The birds are moving farther from the Arctic in order to find food.

owls often travel great distances when they migrate. But they usually stay in the Arctic region. During an irruption, the snowys leave the Arctic. Scientists are not sure what is causing the irruption. Many believe that owls are traveling farther looking for food in the winter months, when hunting is more difficult in the Arctic.

Few humans live in the tundra. This means snowys are not used to dealing with humans. During an irruption, snowys have to learn to make their way in the human world. They do not always succeed. Some snowys have been hit by cars or airplanes.

A person holds a snowy owl that was hit by a bus in Washington, DC.

Making It Last

Snowy owls can go 40 days without food.

CHANGING THREATS

Our planet is getting warmer. This is called climate change. Many animals in the Arctic are affected by climate change. Melting sea ice has caused polar bears to move inland. Usually, the bears do not eat owls. But this has changed as the bears have been cut off from seals, their usual food. Lemmings also rely on snow to make their homes. Warmer temperatures mean less snow and fewer lemmings. This means less food for snowys.

Snowys need snow for **camouflage**. As male owls get older, their feathers lose their black and brown spots. Some of them turn

Snowy owls depend on the white snow to stay hidden from predators. As global warming increases, snow and ice decrease.

completely white. This helps them hide from prey as they sit and scan the tundra. Without snow, the white birds stand out. Humans must work to stop climate change and protect the Arctic habitat. The lives of animals like the snowy owl depend on it.

ACTIVITY

ROLES AT THE POLES

Everything in an ecosystem is connected. A food web shows all the ways plants and animals in an ecosystem connect to each other. A basic food web is shown on page 23.

You have just learned about the snowy owl and how it lives in the Arctic. What else lives there? Read over the list of Arctic animals.

ANIMALS AND MARINE LIFE OF THE ARCTIC

- Snowy owls
- Lemmings
- Moles
- Voles
- Rabbits
- Arctic fox
- Grey wolf
- Skua
- Seals
- Polar bears

Think about what those animals eat. What does a snowy owl eat? What eats the snowy owl? You may need to do some research. Finally, make a food web (like the example shown). Show as many connections as you can.

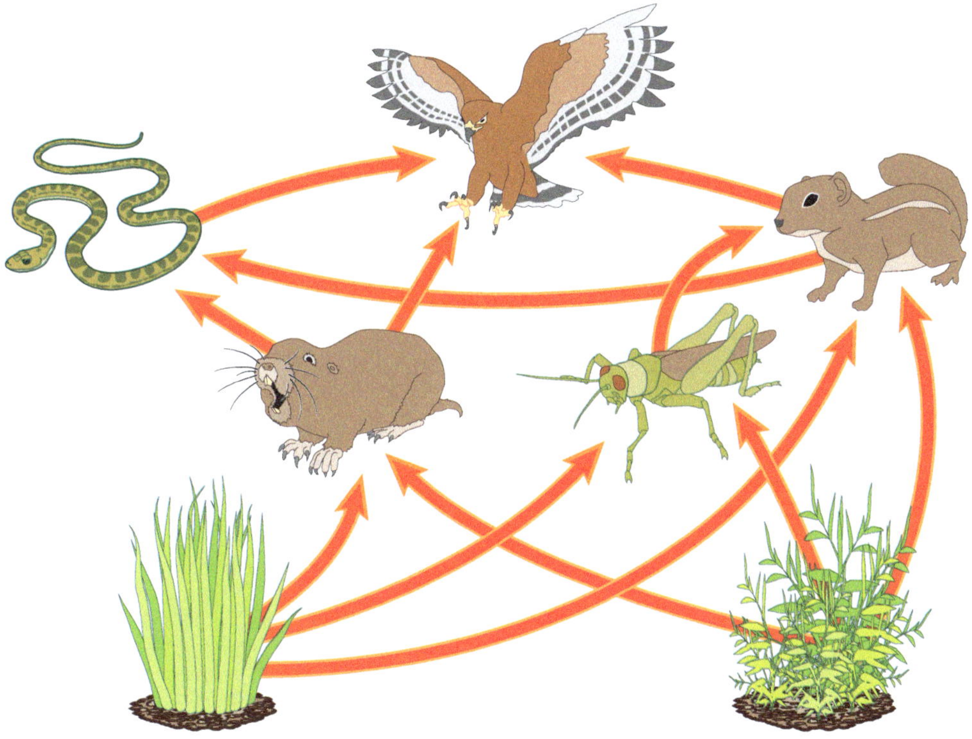

Living things gain energy when they eat. In a food web, arrows point in the direction the energy flows. The grasshopper gets energy from plants and the hawk gets energy from eating the snake.

Learn More

BOOKS

Hirsch, Rebecca E. *Snowy Owls: Stealthy Hunting Birds*. New York, NY: Lerner, 2016.

Lawrence, Riley. *Snowy Owls of the Tundra*. New York, NY: Kidhaven, 2017.

Markle, Sandra. *Snowy Owl Invasion! Tracking an Unusual Migration*. New York, NY: Millbrook Press, 2018.

WEBSITES

National Geographic Kids: Snowy Owls
kids.nationalgeographic.com/animals/snowy-owl/#snowy-owl-closeup.jpg
Learn more about snowy owls and their habitat.

Birds Flight: Snowy Owl Facts for Kids
birdsflight.com/snowy-owl-facts-kids-snowy-owl-facts-diet/
Check out fun facts and photos of the snowy owl.

Index

Published in 2020 by Enslow Publishing, LLC.
101 W. 23rd Street, Suite 240, New York, NY 10011

Library of Congress Cataloging-in-Publication Data

Names: Santos, Rita, author.
Title: Snowy owls / Rita Santos.
Description: New York : Enslow Publishing, 2020. | Series: Life at the Poles | Audience: Grade K-4. | Includes bibliographical references and index. Identifiers: LCCN 2019013442| ISBN 9781978512238 (library bound) | ISBN 9781978512214 (paperback) | ISBN 9781978512221 (6 pack) Subjects: LCSH: Snowy owl--Juvenile literature. Classification: LCC QL696.S83 S27 2020 | DDC 598.9/7--dc23 LC record available at https://lccn.loc.gov/2019013442

Printed in the United States of America

Photos Credits: Snowy Owls – Research by Bruce Donnola

Cover, p. 1 RT Images/Shutterstock.com; p. 5 FotoRequest/Shutterstock.com; p. 6 © iStockphoto.com/pchoui; p. 7 Anatoliy Lukich/Shutterstock.com; p. 9 Wulong Tommy/Shutterstock.com; p. 10 AnnaSmirnova/Shutterstock.com; pp. 12, 18 Vicki Jauron, Babylon and Beyond Photography/Moment/Getty Images; p. 14 Bruce Corbett/Alamy Stock Photo; p. 15 © Paul Blackley/Moment Open/Getty Images; p. 16 Winfried Wisniewski/Corbis/Getty Images; p. 19 The Washington Post/Getty Images; p. 21 © iStockphoto.com/rpbirdman; p. 23 Emre Terim/Shutterstock.com; cover and interior pages (frost pattern) polygraphus/Shutterstock.com